S0-BFD-455

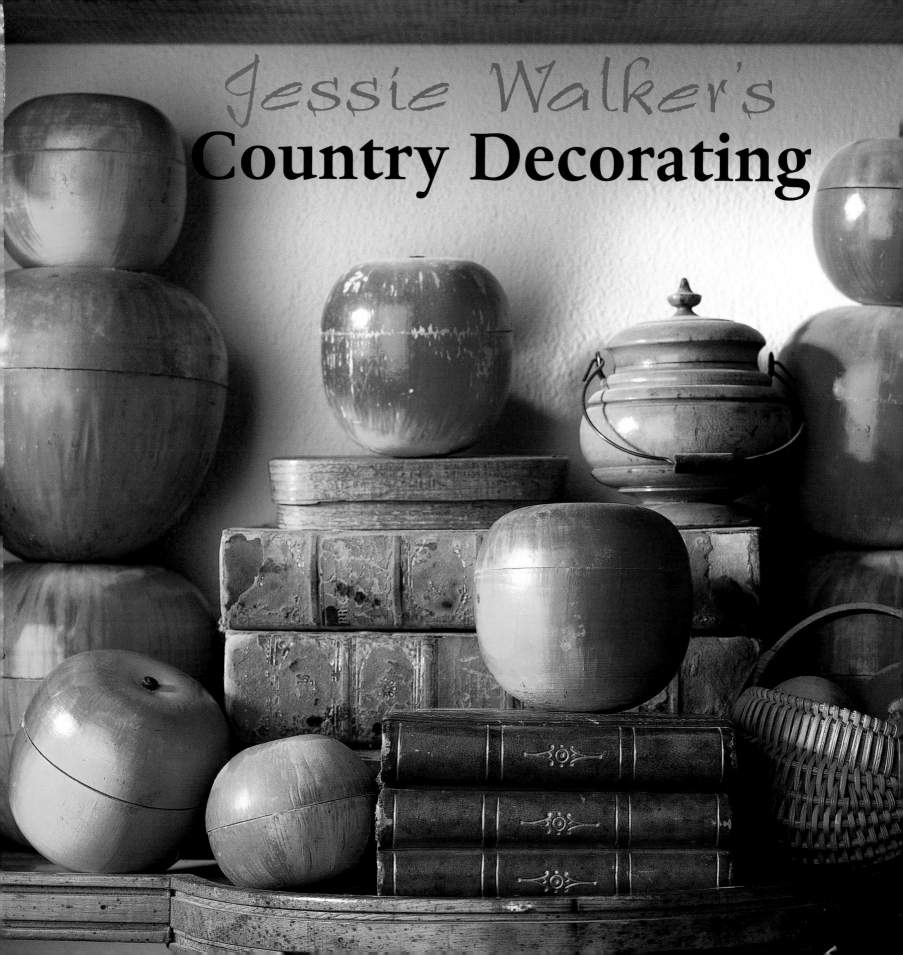

Jessie Walker's
Country Decorating

Jessie Walker's Country Decorating

Sterling Publishing Co., Inc. New York
A Sterling/Chapelle Book

Chapelle, Ltd.:
Jo Packham
Sara Toliver
Cindy Stoeckl

Editor: Lana Hall
Art Director: Karla Haberstich
Copy Editor: Marilyn Goff

Staff: Kelly Ashkettle, Areta Bingham, Anne Bruns, Donna Chambers,
Emily Frandsen, Susan Jorgensen, Jennifer Luman, Melissa Maynard,
Barbara Milburn, Lecia Monsen, Suzy Skadburg, Kim Taylor,
Linda Venditti, Desirée Wybrow

If you have any questions or comments, please contact:
Chapelle, Ltd., Inc., P.O. Box 9252, Ogden, UT 84409
(801) 621-2777 • (801) 621-2788 Fax
e-mail: chapelle@chapelleltd.com
web site: www.chapelleltd.com

The copy, photographs, and designs in this volume are intended for the
personal use of the reader and may be reproduced for that purpose only. Any other
use, especially commercial use, is forbidden under law without the written permission
of the copyright holder.

Every effort has been made to ensure that all information in this book is
accurate. However, due to differing conditions, tools, and individual skills, the
publisher cannot be responsible for any injuries, losses, and/or other damages which
may result from the use of the information in this book.

This volume is meant to stimulate decorating ideas. If readers are unfamiliar
or not proficient in a skill necessary to attempt a project, we urge that they refer to an
instructional book specifically addressing the required technique.

Library of Congress Cataloging-in-Publication Data
Walker, Jessie.
Jessie Walker's country decorating.
p. cm.
"A Sterling/Chapelle book."
Includes index.
ISBN 1-4027-1056-9
1. Decoration and ornament, Rustic. 2. Interior decoration. I. Title: Country
decorating. II. Title.
NK1986.R8W35 2004
747--dc22
                                    2003027774

10 9 8 7 6 5 4 3 2 1

Published by Sterling Publishing Co., Inc.
387 Park Avenue South, New York, NY 10016
©2004 by Jessie Walker
Distributed in Canada by Sterling Publishing
c/o Canadian Manda Group, One Atlantic Avenue, Suite 105
Toronto, Ontario, Canada M6K 3E7
Distributed in Great Britain by Chrysalis Books Group PLC, The Chrysalis
Building, Bramley Road, London W10 6SP, England
Distributed in Australia by Capricorn Link (Australia) Pty. Ltd.
P. O. Box 704, Windsor, NSW 2756, Australia
Printed and Bound in China
All Rights Reserved

Sterling ISBN 1-4027-1056-9

Table of Contents

Introduction

As a photographer, my adventures include capturing Country homes on film in the United States and in England, France, Germany, and Norway. A common thread emerges: Country homes are most often uniquely individual, expressing a special relaxed feeling of warmth, comfort, and hospitality. Their owners feel free to follow their hearts, perhaps in surrounding themselves with time-tested furniture and accessories that please their own sensibilities and speak to their souls. Country homes are never finished. They are often a work in progress being enriched with inspired changes in arrangement, objects, or color.

The look can range from period to rustic or eclectic. There are no hard-and-fast rules for a Country home. It is a place with a special mood that expresses the welcoming approach that seems to say, "Come in and stay." Some are filled with treasures that have been in the family for years, but more often they are alive with a more recently acquired mixture of old and new. Artisans and craftspeople today are hand-fashioning new furniture and accessories inspired by pleasing designs that have remained valid for many years.

You may live in a classic, aging farmhouse tucked into the side of a hill overlooking a meadow with horses, a contemporary suburban ranch close to neighbors with similar houses, or even a sleek high-rise perched in the clouds above a city. Regardless of the limits or the shape of your indoor and outdoor space, you can put together a home with a joyful Country look, adapting many of the ideas illustrated in this book to help you along the way. You will achieve the look with your favorite colors, textures, comfortable furniture, and well-displayed accessories.

When a collection finds you, it will make your environment even more personal. You may be drawn to a Country icon such as Tea Leaf patterned ironstone or you may find that collecting toy boats excites and fascinates your imagination. Perhaps you will become an enthusiastic collector of Depression Glass for a while and then refine your collection with one particular pattern such as pink or green Block Optic, deep cobalt blue Moderntone or, translucent American Sweetheart. Whatever you collect, it will add character and an even deeper personal feel to your home. For impact, group your beloved objects on walls, mantels, tabletops, or in bowls, shelves, or special cabinets for display.

If your outdoor space is limited, you will find ideas such as planting your garden in a vintage wheelbarrow or adding interest with several handcrafted birdhouses, both new and antique, on poles. You can find new uses for discarded pieces of furniture or bring birds to your breakfast-room window by adding a birdbath.

To find special things to amplify your country theme, shop the craft shows featuring the fine distinctive work of skilled artisans and craftsmen. Peruse the Internet. Visit flea markets. Examine the cast-off treasures in your grandparent's attics. Tune in to your Country desires and you will come upon often hard-to-find background materials, furniture, and accessories that will delight and satisfy.

Jessie Walker

Country Style

$\mathcal{P}$eriod Style

When discussing Period Styles in relation to Country decorating, *period* is an era or time in history that you have selected as the basis for your style. It is usually the most formal of the Country decorating styles and is a consistent decorating style, faithfully employing the design and colors of the era selected. After you have completed your research on your selected period style, learn about the woods used, finishes, and characteristic motifs. Consider color, line, texture, and form. Then employ those aspects that appeal to you most in your decorating scheme.

✪ (Far left) When decorating with period pieces, reinvent them to fit your current needs. A period piece, such as a tavern table, can take on another life as a coffee table. Sturdy coffin benches can become decorative and useful end tables. ✪ (Left) This William and Mary period (1690–1730) highboy employed the new technique of gluing an exotic-looking burled veneer to pine planking. The change of building methods fostered a freedom in design, which spawned the golden age of cabinetmaking in America. A taste for tall compressed shapes developed. The banister-back armchair features a bar to hold a baby in place. Pewter plate, candle molds, tall goblets, and treen are all from the period.

Primitive Country Style

Primitive Country style is a remembrance of a simpler way of life. It is a decorating style that is an authentic reflection of the everyday lives of regular people. Because it was the most plentiful material, wood dominates in furniture pieces and accessories, both of which were constructed from utilitarian needs. This plus the untrained craftsperson's aesthetic sensibility helped to determine the designs that are found so appealing today.

✪ (On page 14) With pristine simplicity all elements in the primitive dining room are important to the look of the whole. The worn paint on the double-slat farm chairs and aging table is essential to the charm of the space. Original paint should be enjoyed, not removed. Exposed chinking between the logs is dyed natural to unify the backdrop. Raised paneling on the doors of the blue wall cabinet introduces a restrained embellishment. Notice the wooden latch. ✪ (Above) Everything in the dining room was made by hand, including the pierced-tin chandelier over the farm table and chairs painted black to preserve the wood. ✪ (Right) The loosely interlaced frame of the splint basket hanging on the dining-room wall creates ever-changing shadow patterns on the wall. The screened-front cabinet suggests its original use in the kitchen.

Western Country Style

Western Country Style embodies all of the materials and symbols of the American West. It employs rough natural materials: rocks, leather, metal, logs, twigs, roots, hand-hewn boards, horns, and antlers. The cowboy theme, reminders of Native American art and life, is ever present. Knots, burls, and the natural curve of a log become part of the design of a hand-carved bed or chair. Massive settees and chairs made from the horns of longhorn steers are authentic Western creations. In the 1880s, Texas horn furniture was inspired by Wenzel Friedrich's (1827–1902) prize-winning original designs. The innovative and much-copied legendary Thomas Molesworth (1900–1977) fashioned sturdy Lodge Style, Western furniture out of indigenous materials including burled pine poles, decorating them with cowboy and Native American motifs of the Arts & Crafts movement.

✪ (On page 16 and above) The rugged wood-carved mountainman newel post, tall cowboy boots on the mantel, and Native American drum reborn as an end table, all say Western style. The Western motif is repeated in the hand-loomed throws, lamp bases made from wooden wagon-wheel hubs, vintage leather saddle with brass studs straddling a banister, carved totem pole, ottoman with an antler base, mounted moose head on the wall above the doorway, sconce with metal cowhand portrait, and chandeliers with cut-out metal figures depicting buffalo and men on horseback. The highly polished copper bowl and fireplace surround are elegant accents.

Rustic Style

Rustic Style, born of hardship and necessity, is unpretentious, connecting deeply with the natural world. Homes built of hand-hewn logs, beams and posts, and wide plank flooring are a reminder of American pioneer days. In exchange for room and board, an itinerant untrained artisan or craftsperson, traveling on horseback or wagon, would fashion furniture using local woods. When employing indigenous gutsy materials, the results are honest and straightforward with a simple utilitarian beauty. Many self-reliant settlers shaped their own kitchen implements such as butter paddles, churns, brooms, cheese hoops, bread troughs, and ladles. A local blacksmith made wrought-iron trivets, pot hooks, and cooking forks. The coppersmith made pots, pans, and kettles, while the tinsmith was responsible for lighting fixtures, pierced cabinet door fronts, and kitchen tools.

Cottage Style

Cottage Style is rooted in the vacation home, conjuring up memories of easy-going casual summer holidays. Daydream about a simple seaside dwelling near a sandy beach, or dinner around the fireplace in a north-woods cabin after a renewing hike along an abandoned logging trail. Each of us holds a different vision of Cottage Style. As a second home, it is frequently furnished with mismatched castoffs no longer needed in the year-round house. It is filled with layers of possessions added one piece at a time over a period of years. What began as an unintended style for a romantic part-time home has evolved into a significant style bringing a tranquil atmosphere to year-round homes everywhere.

✿ (Left) Open shelves in a Cottage Style kitchen welcome a reach into the cookie jar, which is always in view. The thoughtfully collected assembly of nostalgic vintage food tins, patterned-metal lunch boxes, worn wooden and metal toys, and cookie molds speak of a happy place. Even the white wooden finials at the corners of the three bottom shelves are a delightful lighthearted touch. ✿ (Above) Bright, light blue cabinets, painted toys, and a woven basket of garden flowers hanging on the door reinforce the Cottage theme of this lighthearted kitchen. Even the ceramic tiles glued onto the backsplash echo the casual feel.

$\mathcal{F}$rench Country Style

French Country, fresh and sophisticated, is a timeless favorite. When local craftsmen living in the provinces of France imitated furniture seen in Paris, a unique Country style developed. Some woods were left in their natural walnut, beech, fruit tree, or oak, while others were washed and painted in pastels with fruit and floral stencil designs.

The well-established guild system requiring a strenuous apprenticeship program lasting from six to eight years produced skilled artisans. This training, coupled with the abundance of native forests, was essential to the development of a sturdy distinctive style, loved for its raw honesty and imaginative flair. Most pieces were a less ornate, pared down version of the furniture that was popular in Paris. Unlike the highly polished imported mahogany, the native woods in a satin finish were more forgiving.

There is an unconscious beauty in a simple settee with a curved back and a woven-rush seat, or a graceful side chair with natural caning. They remain part of the equation even though the invention of coil springs in the mid eighteenth century assured more comfortable seating. Although Country furniture and accessories were produced in all 14 provinces, those from Normandy, Brittany, and Provence highlight the style.

Colors, taking their cue from the countryside and ranging from both earthy and bright sunshine yellows, warm glowing golds, browns, tans, black, and spring green to brilliant cobalt blue, are essential to the palette. Dominant colors vary from region to region. Handwrought wireware, faience such as Quimper, and floral and plain enamelware duplicate this color theme.

✪ (Right) The family room spells welcome. The luxurious print-covered sofas with an abundance of loosely tossed pillows invite relaxation. The thoughtful nonchalance of the mismatched dinner plates, the green enamelware bread box, books for browsing, and the pair of pepper plants add dimension.

Eclectic Style

More Country homes are Eclectic than any other style. Studded with favorite antiques and collectibles, usually gathered over many years and tied together by a common thread, each room evolves into a delightfully distinctive space. Just as no two snowflakes are alike, the uniqueness of Eclectic sets one Country home apart from all the rest. Completely free of any design dictates, Eclectic derives its charm from one's individual panache. A coffee table fashioned from a chicken coop, a hanging plant dangling gracefully from a brass measuring scale, or a battered wooden-crate wall shelf filled with flea-market finds can showcase this special inimitable style. Exclusive by its very nature, Eclectic speaks a language all its own.

✪ (Right) Cypress-twig garden furniture brought indoors, abundant greenery, a wooden horse once used in a Maryland saddle shop, a pair of painted wooden Native Americans by a Georgia carver, a totem pole and an array of collectibles combine for a warm, welcoming Eclectic room.

Shaker Style

Shaker Style reflects the spiritual beliefs of this communal religious sect. They sought to make their lives echo the beauty and perfection of God's heaven. Their emphasis on order and neatness is represented in the simple utilitarian design of their architecture, furniture, tools, and accessories. Fine craftsmanship dominates. With its clean lines and lack of ornamentation, furniture was light, sturdy, and easy to clean. Their desire for harmony included the sharing of inventions and ideas. Shakers, named for their whirling religious dance, gave the world the flat broom, circular saw, swivel chair, seed packets, clothespins, and much more. Written orders for living their lives and the standards for building and furniture design emanated from the society headquarters on Mount Lebanon, New York. The 1821 orders were revised in 1845 and throughout the nineteenth century. Shaker life hit its zenith from 1840 to 1850. It declined after the Civil War.

✿ (Left) Wood peg rails, a Shaker icon used for hanging chairs, garments, hats, baskets, tools, clocks, and candleholders promote all-important order and cleanliness. Mushroom-shaped handmade wooden pegs remain the most characteristic. Items hung on the wall clear the floor for sweeping. Because celibacy was a Shaker tenant, single beds were the rule. ✿ (Upper right) This spiral staircase is the focal point in the Trustees' office at Shakertown Pleasant Hill, Kentucky. ✿ (Lower right) The distinctive design of the Shaker's wood-burning stove was efficient and visually pleasing. The iron chamber of the stove and its long chimney radiated heat in all directions making fireplaces unnecessary. Drawers built into the walls reinforce the need for order.

Country Color

Red, White & Blue Combinations

Country color combinations are limitless, bounded only by one's imagination. For many years, muted colors alone were associated with Country. More recently, the palette has been expanded to include superb blends of lighter, frequently brighter colors. Faithfully restored historic homes reveal vivid colors used by our ancestors. Without modern chemistry, paints on their architectural gems had faded, giving them a softer and sometimes sober look. Original colors, once discovered, were brought back to their former intensity. The comfort of the familiar red, white, and blue might provide the deepest sense of Country. Numerous accessories such as a fire screen, checkerboard, flag, war bond sign, and wooden Uncle Sam figures reinforce a traditional theme.

Barn Red

Pulsating bold red in all its range of hues and tints conveys friendliness. It dominates when generously used and provides a spunky accent when added in small doses. Neat red-and-white checkered wallpaper and solid scarlet red dinner plates, shown at left, stimulate the appetite. Because red energizes as it creates the festive air of abundance, it is wonderful in kitchens and family, dining, and breakfast rooms.

✪ (Upper left on page 33) Red never retreats, yet its drama is successfully subdued when tempered by white. The crisp white background of the floral-patterned plates and the white of the Staffordshire dog on the wall shelf in a dining room tone down the intensity of the scene. Soft pink reds are romantic. ✪ (Upper right on page 33) Rich country reds are frequently calm in darker hues such as wine or deep maroon, with a slightly weathered feel. More than any other color, shades of red are affected by daylight. They fade quickly as the gentle glow of evening overtakes a sunny afternoon. ✪ (Lower left on page 33) The generous use of white in the quilt offsets the intense passionate red of the painted chest of drawers. Because red is a pure color, all of its hues work well together as illustrated by the red in the antique quilt, the dark red of the weathered country bench, and the berry red of the antiqued chest. ✪ (Lower right on page 33) Bright cherry red is especially brilliant against a green background. Red and green are on opposite sides of the color wheel, making them complementary colors. As a pure primary color, red cannot be made by combining colors. It can be lightened or darkened progressively by using varying amounts of white or black.

Country White

White, along with its companions, cream, tan, taupe, gray, brown, and black, is the natural component of a gentle soothing background. These neutrals, in their infinite variety of shades and textures, surround us in the world outside. Witness the puffy white to stormy gray clouds in the sky, the mixture of course to fine pebbles and sand on a beach, the gradation of stone hues in a quarry, and the slim to massive tree trunks everywhere. White is enduring, luxurious, chic, restful, and serene. There is nearly monastic simplicity in an interior that is a montage of neutrals. People themselves become the color accents.

✪ (Below) The very closeness of neutrals to the world outside gives them a special affinity to Country. Warm weathered-wood furniture in browns or grays looks great against a backdrop in shades of white on walls. In this living room, shades of white, tan, brown, and black are thoughtfully assembled with each element serving a purpose both practical and visual. Sofas and chairs are covered in an off-white canvas duck. A drop-leaf tavern table with shortened legs is now a coffee table providing serving space. Vintage brown stoneware jugs are reborn as lamps. Carefully placed accessories are kept to a minimum, making each one important. ✪ (On page 35) In the dining room, gray-white fabric balls in the antique treen bowl, the tin sconce, the pierced-tin chandelier, and a pair of wooden checkerboards establish the theme. The distressed-wood finishes of the worn farm table and bow-backed Windsor armchairs feel perfect together.

Classic Blue

Blue is a much loved Country color, associated with loyalty and commitment. Just as we can count on a "true-blue" person to stand with us in times of need, the color blue is classic, making it a safe choice for any room. Walls, woodwork, furniture, fabrics, and accessories in one or more of the infinite blues define the atmosphere of a space. The built-in Georgian Style hutch, shown on page 36, is painted a washed Colonial blue, generating a powerful bond with our historic past.

Blue, in all its shades and tints, fosters a calm casual mood. As one of the three primary colors, it cannot be created by mixing other colors. Blue used with white is light and airy. Darker serious shades spell tradition.

Warm Green

Green is a mixture of blue and yellow. When there is more blue than yellow, the color will be cool. Conversely, when yellow dominates, the resulting green will be warm.

✪ (Lower left) The tulips are especially vivid in contrast with the complementary green directly across the color wheel. ✪ (Lower right) Darker greens suggest calm and quiet. Lighter hues are lively and refreshing. The white to cream chalk figures empower the dark gray-green recessed shelves, giving them a cool strength. ✪ (On page 39) Serious dark Colonial green paint with a distressed finish is combined with a muted dark red island and stained wide-plank pine floors to promote an authentic Country look. Even a dark green will link an interior color with the exterior where nature's greens abound.

Sunshine Yellow

The most luminous of all colors, true cadmium yellow is the standard brilliant sunshine. Add white to lighten it to lemon yellow, as shown at left, or black to darken it to mustard yellow, as shown on page 41. Because yellow is a naturally light-toned color, the deeper shades tend toward orange, green, and brown. The earthy brown and green bowls are in harmony with the mustard-colored walls and woodwork. The muted darker yellow has been linked with Country since Colonial days.

✪ (Lower left) The pale straw-yellow drawers are warm without becoming overpowering. This soft yellow expresses its easy sense of hospitality making it a successful Country color. ✪ (Lower right) The slightly brighter primrose yellow is a cheerful backdrop for an eating area. The contrasting blue-patterned pottery brightens the congenial setting.

$\mathcal{V}$ibrant Mixture

A vibrant mixture of eleven contrasting and relating colors, as shown above, adds drama to a narrow hallway in a 125-year-old farmhouse. Vintage sap buckets in shades of yellow, blue, green, orange, red, and purple are stacked on an antique washstand painted barn red. The neutral-tan scrolled stairway trim relieves the intense feeling of the dark navy blue walls.

Experiment with groupings when combining a potpourri of color. The divers patterns in the kitchen area, shown on page 43, are unified by relating colors. The deep red of the floral-patterned cushions on the rocking chairs and the orange red geometric-patterned wallpaper tie the floral and the geometric together.

Fabulous Fabrics

✪ (Above) Once consigned underfoot, these cherished hooked-wool pieces become proudly displayed as objets d'art. A late-nineteenth-century Country runner combining stylized floral design with geometric patterns, draped over the door between the dining room and the kitchen in this Missouri farmhouse, beckon all to enter. It is a source of everyday pleasure.

Hooked Rugs

The strong presence of a hand-hooked rug is a Country home essential. Hard wall surfaces, softened by these graceful pieces with their naive charm, offer comfort like a warm bowl of soup on a cold day. There is a striking similarity in design in antique rugs because most rug hookers used commercial patterns. In 1868, a Maine peddler named Edward Sands Frost made sheet-metal stencils for leaves, flowers, scrolls, and animals, combining them in different patterns for sale. The 1895 Montgomery Ward catalog offered 15 designs. Old rugs are pictorial, showing people, animals, ships, and houses as well as floral and geometric patterns. Because the design of a hooked rug is more important to its value than its age, those made by today's artisans are usually more unique and desirable. Before hanging, rugs should be professionally mounted.

✪ (Below, upper right, and right) The cat, Saltbox-style house, and horse are all well-loved themes in hooked rugs. Tears and bald spots in an antique rug can be repaired. If it sheds a fine dust, the "ground" of the rug may be deteriorating and it cannot be rescued.

Pillows

Successful decorating is in the details. Fabrics in limitless colors, weaves, textures, and patterns are available to encase pillows of endless shapes and sizes. Soft and comfy, pillows will intensify the welcoming spirit of your home. A firm pillow will provide back support on a sofa that may be too deep.

✪ (On page 48) The pillowed sofa and settee breathe comfort and beauty into this sunny family room. The pleasing time-tested mixture of provincial prints illustrate the abundance of patterns and complementary colors that work well together. The fluffy fringe on some of the pillows softens the scene even more. ✪ (Left) The color blue is the unifying element of this artful arrangement of pillows on a wicker settee. Each pillow is given individuality with its own fabric, pattern, shape, size, and trim. Notice the fanciful cat-shaped pillow tucked in between the square and round pillows. ✪ (Lower right) A lush mélange of pillows draws the eye to the head of the bed. The checkered, striped, polka-dot, and floral patterns all relate in color. Embellished with pretty floral motifs, pillows become accent pieces in a bedroom, breakfast room, sunroom, or porch.

Kitchen Linens

Softly faded kitchen and table linens from the early 1940s through the 1970s speak to us with the authentic and natural voice of Country.

Tablecloths printed with flower and fruit themes may be cotton sheeting, sailcloth, or even linen. Colors range from an alluring fairy-tale pink to a gray blue or deep magenta. In addition to tablecloths, there are hand towel linens whose colors are more natural and whose designs vary from subtle sophisticated hotel stripes to kitschy '50s art.

Such kitchen linens can be used in today's Country decorating for many things. Hand towels become oversized napkins, tablecloths are now café curtains, napkins are sewn together into place runners or chair seat cushions. It matters not that they are aged and worn, such wear only adds to a nostalgic country style.

✪ (On page 50) The personal way of combining and displaying vintage linens will tell family and friends what is loved. A spare room may provide an extra bed to cluster colorful stacks. The look is casual and easygoing. A panoply of textured red-and-white towels, bedspreads, and tea cloths can be hung on the arms of an antique clothes dryer. ✪ (Right) Collectible hat boxes culled from a flea market will provide storage for fabric scraps awaiting a future project. A peg rail supplies more hanging space for a variety of retro laundry bags. When planning a room, think of inventive ways to amass and display treasures. Handmade Turkey redwork, a crisp white linen with a distinctive red-and-white stitch similar to crewel, blends well with others in the same color scheme with various textures, sizes, and patterns.

Quilts

Colorful handmade quilts, folded and stacked, hung on a wall, used as a bedspread, tucked away in an armoire, or thrown across a sofa, will give an immediate inviting Country look to a home. They can be pieced quilts in an established or innovative pattern, crazy quilts fashioned from a random assortment of more formal fabrics, or plain quilts with the whole top and bottom made from an unbroken piece of fabric and a cotton batting filling.

✪ (On page 52) Antique 1880s crazy quilts mingle with several log-cabin quilts and others with nonspecific designs. ✪ (Lower left) Quilts with delicate stitching are considered especially desirable. Of course, age, quality of materials, colors, and rare patterns are important to the connoisseur. ✪ (Upper right) The Circles, or Mill Wheel, quilt in red and gray hangs over a log railing. ✪ (Lower right) The strong pattern and rich color of the 1910 Amish Ocean Waves quilt is visually exciting on the wall, as is the folded 1915 Courthouse Steps quilt at the foot of the bed and the 1925 Pinwheel quilt used as a spread.

53

Coverlets

Coverlets are Country classics which add authenticity to the Country theme. Woven of wool and linen or cotton, the earliest examples, with bold geometric designs such as those from the 1820s, shown at right, were used to decorate beds in the nineteenth and twentieth centuries.

Wool was the easiest handwoven fabric to dye. In 1805, a device known as a Jacquard loom, named after inventor Joseph Marie Jacquard of Lyons, France, made more-complex designs, even floral patterns with multiple colors, possible.

The Jacquard loom used punch cards to determine the pattern of cloth woven on a hand loom and was later used on steam-powered weaving machines as well. By 1812, some 11,000 Jacquards were being used in Europe.

Jacquards were used in the United States only briefly. By the end of the Civil War, competition from factory-made bedding practically eliminated handwoven coverlets from the market.

When they became too worn or tattered for use on a bed, early coverlets were given other uses, such as horse blankets or to protect produce on its way to the market. Coverlets remaining today are those that were tenderly cared for.

✪ (On page 54) The antique coverlet hung over the high back of a settler's bench and the neat square puffy pillows encased with woven geometric design fabric both complement the barn-red wall paneling and soften the hard wood setting. ✪ (Upper right) Traditional navy blue and cream-colored coverlets warm weary sleepers nestled in these antique rope beds. Part of the allure of a coverlet is its versatility; incorporating both practical and beauty. ✪ (Lower right) One can extend the life of the cover and achieve a new look by reversing the piece. Note the altered ambience created by white on blue and blue on white.

Penny Rugs

Country celebrates the handmade. There is something intimate and nurturing about living with things made by hand. Penny rugs will warm a home and enrich life. We are curious about the nineteenth-century schoolgirl, who learned necessary sewing skills by making lightweight and fragile penny rugs from scraps of wool and felt. Using the large copper penny of the period as a template, dozens of circles were cut out and then fastened to a coarse backing, such as a seed bag, with a blanket stitch. Some were embroidered or appliquéd. To make felt (which will not ravel) wool (which shrinks as it dries) was washed in hot water and then pressed before cutting. Geometric patterns are endless. Because of their delicate nature, penny rugs make effective table toppers or wall hangings. Rugs made by overlapping and stitching tongues of felt, such as that hanging over the chair back, as shown below, are another variation.

57

Homespun

Homespun fabric with its feel of natural fibers and soothing muted colors captures the values of Country Style. Linen, cotton, and wool, spun and woven at home, were eighteenth- and nineteenth-century necessities. Today's skilled crafters are reinforcing a link with the past by repeating the same process. Looms in many styles are available as are warping tools, shuttles, and bobbins.

✪ (On page 58) This four-poster bed, invitingly dressed in soft yellow and muted striped homespun, frames a peg rail hung with late-nineteenth-century autumnal-colored fabrics. Admired for their simplicity of design, most homespun fabrics are plain or have a checkered pattern. Indigo blues are the most common colors, while browns and yellows, because their acidic dyes broke down the fabrics, are rare today. ✪ (Left and below) Antique homespun in blue-and-white checkers and stripes is loved and readily available. Indigo blue, extracted from indigo and woad plants, was the most popular and durable dye. ✪ (Above) Fine reproduction fabrics are plentiful. Three blankets and an Amish linen overdyed with walnut husks hang in an upstairs hall because direct sunlight deteriorates the textiles. The tall antique doll complements the second doll and dog, both reproductions.

Samplers

Needlework samplers are a true Country icon. As the only important collectible created by children, they bring history back to life, revealing an unmatched intimacy. In the eighteenth and nineteenth centuries, samplers were schoolroom projects. Young girls, given lessons in basic needlework, would master the craft of stitching samplers to showcase their handiwork. At times, teachers would dictate the subject, which could include the alphabet, poetry, or verses from the Bible. The most interesting and unique samplers were creations by the girls themselves. Highly prized antique pieces have human figures, trees, animals, houses, or Bible scenes, all in color along with the name and age of the stitcher. Those that do not remain in a family where they have been passed down from generation to generation are usually on display in museums.

✪ (On page 60) Hand-stitched samplers grouped on the wall of a stairway were reproduced from seventeenth-century museum originals. Kits are faithful copies of scarce antiques. With a variety of frames and sampler sizes and shapes, it is important to create a cohesive arrangement by spacing the individual pieces close together.

✪ (Above) This reproduction sampler of Noah's Ark exhibits a joyous mixture of verse, color, and needlework. This scenic piece is especially treasured for decorative quality. The long and narrow shape is unusual. Samplers with straight-from-the-heart sentiments are calming in Country homes.

Painted Pleasure

sure

$\mathcal{P}$aints

Paint simply and easily accomplishes an unlimited spectrum of style and mood and is especially essential in providing a distinctively Country look in any setting. Brushed, stenciled, sponged, or stippled finishes in pastoral hues lovingly imbue a home with unique personality.

Paint protects and beautifies while enhancing anything it touches. Lavish the walls with washes of Country color, highlight moldings with richly shaded pigments, mottle furnishings with tinted glazes, or accent accessories with a soft patina—and the blank canvas that was the room transforms into a welcoming retreat.

✪ (Right and below) Freehand design applied to any surface bestows individual character. An old wooden chair or table dressed with a brightly colored coat of paint and adorned with a whimsical trailing of fruit or flowers will give a room an element of interest as well as endow a family with a treasured heirloom.

✪ (On page 65) Combine paint styles for added visual power. An unwanted, limed oak finish was hand-rubbed to give cabinets a distressed patina. A stenciled border design on a soft yellow painted pantry suggests a Country Style kitchen.

Stencils

Stencils impart an artistic ability to even the most creatively challenged. Affordable, quick and simple stenciling techniques, mastered in less than a day create warm homey Country accents.

Apply patterns in traditional Country designs individually, or mix elements of multiple patterns to add versatility and individuality to a project. Use one of the thousands of precut guides available, or create a design for a unique effect by sketching or tracing the image on stencil blanks available at craft or hobby shops. Carefully cut each element with an artist's utility knife. Set the mood with monochromatic or multicolored designs. Each color of the pattern will require its own stencil.

Just about every surface lends itself to stenciling. Embellish a wood floor or plain painted wall with a stencil border, beautify fireplace or kitchen tiles with mini stencils, highlight a window, or surround a fireplace mantel with the addition of a stenciled frame.

✪ (On page 66) This large foyer handsomely displays bold stenciling. Pick colors that complement other room accents such as the red, blue, and cream of these area rugs. Tie elements together by mimicking graphics such as the central diamond pattern of the rug repeated in the ceiling border. Complement woodwork with a harmonizing hue. ✪ (Right) The smallest space can give a large visual impact. Here a statement was made by stenciling stair risers with a simple arch and daisy pattern, turning the mundane to marvelous.

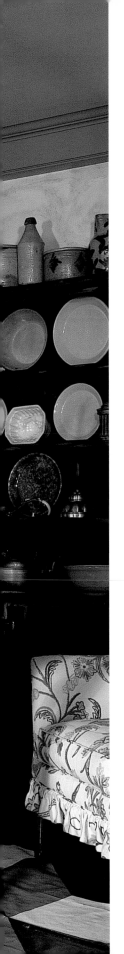

Murals

Wall murals evoke the emotion of a majestic mountainscape, the remote horizon of an ocean view, or the idyllic scenery of a favorite countryside setting. Bringing an outside vista in not only brightens a living space, but also presents an interesting conversation starter.

Much like ancient cave paintings, murals can also tell a story, depicting historic war battles or ancestral voyages to new lands, or visually chronicle a family history. The choice of subject can be as common and simple as a pastoral scene painted above a door or as personal and elaborate as an ancestral saga marching around the entire room.

Make a mural whimsical with quirky, fanciful illustrations of a theme; or use a realistically formal style, there is no rule of style.

69

ʇ rompe l'oeil

French for "fool the eye," trompe l'oeil painting creates an illusion, tricking the viewer into seeing something that really is not there. This home owner brought her fantasy of an imaginary family living in a provincial cottage to life with ingenious faux elements added to both her home and a simple potting shed in her "cottage garden."

✪ (Upper left on page 70) A faux weatherworn garden jacket and a pair of pruning shears hang from pegs, while a straw sunbonnet perches on an ersatz window shutter. ✪ (Lower right on page 70) Sneakers, the bona fide family pet, guards the door fancifully highlighted with trompe l'oeil wood grain and wrought-iron hinges.

✪ (Above) Exaggerated wood patterns such as the tiger maple look recall the rustic finishes of rural painters. Burnt sienna over mustard paint established the base coat, while a rolled-up newspaper developed the thick grain lines. Graining is enhanced by black accent outlines.

grained Woods

Imitation being the sincerest form of flattery, wood graining pays the highest compliment to that which it graces. Graining not only imparts warmth and charm to all that it touches but adds a distinctively special ambience to your Country room.

Even the lowliest grades of wood come to life when clothed with a faux wood-grain finish. Graining combs, rockers, checkered rollers, floggers, or mottlers, dragged, combed, and rocked on base-coated and glazed wooden surfaces create amazingly realistic wood patterns, implying a richness of tradition and history.

Various techniques using wood-graining tools, brushes, and other imaginative implements christen chairs, tables, walls, moldings, and even nonwood surfaces with the characteristic grains of soft pine, sturdy oak, rich cherry, or hard maple. Duplicate lighter-hued woods such as pine or maple by painting an undercoat of yellow or buff. Cherry or mahogany reproduction calls for shades of red. After the topcoat has dried, a coat of glaze is brushed on and then removed with your graining tool of choice. Combining tools, such as a rocker and a comb or comb and flogger, produces different grain characteristics such as knots or burls.

Whitewash

Paneled walls washed in white, revealing hints of grain, suggest the ethereal haze of early morning fog in a meadow. Whitewash used in pioneer cabins, farmhouses, and provincial cottages brightened the poorly lit interiors of yesteryear.

Mixing water into a latex-based white paint or a thinning medium into an oil-based paint produces the primitive translucent quality of whitewash. Control the depth of color by adding more or less of the reducer. A traditional whitewash hue can be attained with a mixture of eight or nine parts reducer to one part paint mixture. Sand or strip a wood surface to remove old finish. Be certain to eliminate all sanding residue before applying the wash. Finish and seal the surface with wax or varnish.

✪ (Above) Fresh whitewash was applied every spring to the rough hewn walls of the Conner Prairie Pioneer Settlement in Indiana. ✪ (Right) The walls of the blacksmith's home and the widow's house are kept in the same pristine condition today as they were when these rooms were home to Indiana pioneers over one hundred and seventy-five years ago. The spinning wheel, large iron pot, wooden scoop, bags hanging on the wall and tin sconce with candle are reminders of life in the nineteenth century.

$\mathcal{D}$istressed Finishes

Prized pieces revealing the cumulative effects of years of exposure to both the tactile and the elements impart genuine Country flavor to any setting. Generations of living reflected on the multilayered surface of a distressed cupboard, table, or bed pull your thoughts back into its history.

Worn layers of paint bequeath an atmosphere of antiquity and a sense of uniqueness to a room's woodwork, paneling, and furnishings. Searching flea markets, house sales, or second-hand shops may unearth a rare find, but carefully applying and randomly removing layers of paints and glazes to wood surface can instantly bestow decades of patina to new or gently used furniture.

A Rustic Country look derives its character from dark base colors, such as burnt umber, sienna, brown, or black. Once the base is thoroughly dried, begin lightly sanding areas of obvious wear, such as the edges of doors, drawers, or behind cabinet pulls, to mimic actual wear and tear. The more irregularly the paint layers are removed, the more natural the finish appears. A finish can be made even more rustic by brushing a crackling medium between two layers of paint or glaze, causing the topcoat to crack and expose the base coat, giving the piece a timeworn look.

✪ (On page 76) If you want a more traditional formal mood, use light bases coated with color-tinted glazes that are immediately dry-brushed off in sweeping uneven lines to look like fine-grained wood and convey a subtle elegance.

Country Ceramics

✪ (Above) Display beloved pieces at eye-level. These early-nineteenth-century pieces are always in view on top of an 1860 pie safe. Their similar color and complementary shapes create a pleasing visual unit.

Redware Pottery

Redware, made of rich red common clay with an iron content, became the most serviceable pottery made everywhere in America until about 1850 when it was replaced by imported whiteware, yellowware, and stoneware. Extremely porous, redware was generally glazed with lead to make it watertight. Unaware of its poisonous lead finish, people used it for food, drink, and storage for almost 100 years.

✪ (Above) Don't hesitate to mix old and new redware. Ohio sgraffito (scratched-in design) plates made by a contemporary potter mingle with 1850s jugs and pitchers on a living-room mantel.

Galena & Brookville Yellowware Pottery

Whether featured as accessories on the coffee table or in neat rows lining the shelves of an open cupboard, yellowware incorporates the Country look.

Loved for its simplicity and soft mellow color, yellowware was the most inexpensive and basic pottery available during nineteenth-century America.

England was the major source until the 1870s when large automated factories with gas-fired kilns increased output in America. From the 1860s through the 1880s, Ohio boasted many of the biggest potteries. Early centers of production developed in New England.

Both utilitarian and graceful, these sturdy bowls are usually banded in white in a variety of widths and bands. They were rarely marked, making it difficult to determine the age or the manufacturer.

Antique yellowware is not hard to find. Authentic reproductions have the same historic appeal as the originals. Museum workshops are a reliable source for new pieces.

✪ (On page 83) Used as a mass, yellowware bowls become important, promoting a sense of purpose and order. They can be distractions if scattered around the room. ✪ (Left) Grouped on shelves in ascending sizes, banded yellowware bowls set the mellow mood in this Country kitchen.

✪ (Above) On an antique bucket bench, lead-glazed pottery made in Galena and Brookville, Illinois, helps to root the room in the past. The lethal nature of lead glaze makes these a feast for the eyes only.

✪ (Above) Antique yellowware behind the protective glass doors of the antique step-back cabinet mixes successfully with one shelf of spongeware decorated in dark blue. The latter was made from a variety of materials, usually stoneware or yellowware. The most important centers of production were East Liverpool, Ohio, and Red Wing, Minnesota. To determine if a piece of yellowware is authentic, turn it over to check that the bare clay on the bottom rim is yellow and not the gray of comparative plain stoneware.

Creative Blends

For visual pleasure, ceramics grouped in divers patterns in an attractive wall-mounted deep blue cabinet, shown at right, include Leeds ware, Gaudy ware, and Salopian ware, all finished in unifying shades of blue and all made in England.

Leeds ware was made in and near Leeds, Yorkshire, (circa 1760–1820) and is of especially fine quality. The name is associated with a thinly potted creamware, often decorated with pierced-work, relief decoration, transfer printing, and polychrome painted decoration, but also could be black basalts, agate, pearl, tortoiseshell, marble, and others.

Eighteenth-century Gaudy Dutch, also called Gaudy Welch, was extravagantly painted with stylized flower patterns. It was made in the west of England for inexpensive markets.

Salopian ware was made at Caughley, near Broseley, Shropshire, in a factory started in 1772 by Thomas Turner and sold in 1799 to John Rose. Much was decorated with an unglazed blue and either painted or transfer-printed.

✪ (Lower right) A relaxed Country mood is achieved in the dining room, by displaying other items with important ceramics. Dominating the scene, Bennington pottery and early-nineteenth-century Chinese exports line shelves with a plain cream-colored background. The watchmaker's trade sign and gold-leaf pharmacy sign hanging on the wall add dimension. The mid-1800s Wisconsin farm table with two hand-carved doves from the early 1900s, wooden spools from old looms, two small birds and an electric lamp converted from an old kerosene lamp are cherished objects giving the room personal meaning. Experimentation can bring success.

$\mathcal{F}$low Blue Pottery

This form of ironstone pottery is called Flow Blue because the color from the transfer-printed pattern flowed onto the undecorated portions of the unglazed earthenware during the glaze firing. Lime or chloride of ammonia was added into the protective shell of the fireclay sagger—the shell in which the vessel is placed during the glaze firing—to cause the flow process. It was ideal for the potting industry because the color bleed hid a myriad of potting imperfections. This look of informality fits with Country themes.

Originally sneered at by British critics, these durable dishes graced many American tables from about 1835 into the first quarter of the twentieth century. Although produced mostly by potters in England, Flow Blue was also made in Scotland and the United States. As underglazing techniques improved, other colors were introduced, such as mulberry, sepia, and pruce, a dark brownish purple. Although mulberry achieved considerable acceptance, blue remained the most popular.

Quimper Pottery

Quimper pottery, handmade in Brittany for over 300 years, will amplify the French Country look of your home. Quimper with a butter-yellow background was first produced in the 1920s. New Quimper faience is available worldwide.

ℱiesta Pottery

Fiesta pottery with its casual style and bright colors became an immediate success upon its introduction by Homer Laughlin in 1936. Its five original colors: red, blue, yellow, green, and ivory, had expanded to 11 colors; and slight styling variations were made before production was ceased for 13 years in 1973. It was reintroduced in 1986 with new colors: cobalt blue (darker than the original), rose (deep pink), white, apricot (pale peach) and black. Some of the pieces were restyled to accommodate a different firing technique and some details were changed to resemble the original line designed by Frederick Hurten Rhead.

✪ (Above and right) Its appealing mixture of colors and Art Deco-inspired design assures Fiesta pottery's place as a favorite in Country homes. Notice the curving and convex shape and concentric band of rings.

$\mathcal{T}$erra-cotta Pottery

Terra-cotta is Italian for "baked earth." It is a hard, semi-fired, absorbent clay that can be used for decorative or functional purposes.

Bowls, plates, pitchers, and a wine jug made of terra-cotta earthenware feel informal and warm in contrast to the formal style and cold hard surface of the delicate crystal stemware.

✪ (Above) Before serving food on earthen-ware, be certain it is approved for food use. ✪ (Left) Express flair for the innovative by the way ceramics are combined. The gentle gray-green pottery, made at the school in Berea, Kentucky, tempers the strong pattern and brilliant colors of the pieces from Sienna, Italy. Each plate, canister, or mug bears a crest from one of the families of Sienna.

$\mathcal{R}$ivera Pottery

Rivera pottery was intended for use in mixed colors, as in this table setting, shown at right. Laughlin Pottery experimented successfully to achieve colors that would go well together.

Their colors were mauve, blue, red, yellow, light green, and ivory. The red is sometimes called bright orange. Rivera is not as durable as its relative Fiesta. It was sold at Woolworth stores (1938 until about 1950) and is both collected and used carefully. It is best to wash it by hand because it chips easily.

This multicolored pottery was made originally in East Liverpool, Ohio, by Laughlin Pottery, formed in 1871 by brothers Homer and Shakespeare Laughlin. The company's products won the highest award at the 1876 Centennial Exposition in Philadelphia.

In 1906, a fourth plant was built in Newell, West Virginia. Plant number five was built in 1913. Plant number six, built in 1923, was equipped with the revolutionary continuous tunnel kiln, a giant step toward mass production. This was so successful that plants number seven and eight were built. The company became a giant concern employing 2,500 workers and is still a principal dinnerware producer in the world today.

Rivera Pottery goes well with the brighter colors of Western Country, the casual feel of Cottage style, the warm sun drenched paints of a French Country style, or the collector's freedom and abandon in an Eclectic Country style.

✪ (Above right and right) Festive Rivera looks well stacked on open shelves or in glass-front cupboards.

Wood & Metal

Wood & Metal

Wood and metal are two elements essential to a Country look. Wonderful wood, with its endlessly adaptable shapes and uses, is appropriate for backgrounds such as floors, walls, and ceilings, for furniture, and for all important accessories. You may crave the patina of aged or distressed lumber, the smooth uniform look of a hardwood such as maple, or the dominating grain of oak. Man-made metal, sometimes used for a background like pressed-tin or copper ceilings, exudes an exciting strength and the same look of durability as an iron bed frame or wire bench. Its reflective qualities usher in a special kind of magic when fashioned into sculpture.

✪ (On page 94) An all-wood room is beautiful in its ambience. The natural-scrubbed surface of the pine table, the chip-carved chairs, the antique pine cupboard with doors enhanced by rose-maling, eighteenth-century mangle boards, and the painted wooden jug and plate live well together. Several metal accessories add dimension.
✪ (Above) The rusty wrought-iron fence and flowers demonstrate the visual impact of contrasting hard metal with the soft greenery behind it.

Treen

Unassuming weathered woods in blending shades of off-white promote a sense of serenity. The 1840 corner cupboard, mid-nineteenth-century dry sink, oversized treen bowl, wood-slat buckets with covers, wide farm table, and side chairs are all carefully chosen antiques. The tin chandelier with candles, vintage copper weather vane in the popular running horse design, rusty watering can, and iron beam braces are pleasing accents.

The look is supremely comfortable. The timeworn whitewashed finish and texture of the dominant furniture, the muted tones in the plaid handwoven rug, and the mismatched wooden chairs say Country. Although thoughtfully planned, the room feels casual and relaxing.

✪ (Below) Wood in neutral tones is the unifying element. An antique textured wooden wall cabinet, stacks of wooden pantry boxes, a wooden wall shelf with earthenware plates, the bow-back Windsor armchair with a distressed finish, and a vintage bucket with a hint of its original blue color remaining combine to create the whole.

Woodenware, or treen, items were necessary for early American settlers. Short on kitchen utensils, bowls, platters, and containers of metal and pottery, many items were fashioned from wood. Maple, ash, birch, pine, and other woods were plentiful in the dense forests. Hard woods like maple and birch were ideal for items such as mortars and pestles, while softer woods were used for spoons and boxes. Utensils could be made cheaply by anyone who could whittle, carve, or use a primitive lathe. A wide variety of items were standard in prerevolutionary American homes, all with the honest appeal of a handmade piece. With time and use, woodenware gains a rich patina, as evidenced in the treen, shown on page 98 and above. Nothing says "Country" more than a collection of mellow, well-worn woodenware.

$\mathcal{M}$etal Medley

Each type of metal speaks in a different voice. Brass—high pitched and formal—works well with period Country. It is an effective trim accent on furniture, lighting fixtures, candlesticks, faucets, hardware, door knockers, garden sundials, or perhaps a baker's rack.

Copper—lower pitched and more resonant—often finds its home with Ethnic and Eclectic Country. It is elegant for roofing and plumbing fixtures. Teapots, kitchen molds, measures, skimmers, jugs, pots, and pans, all made of copper can be used or displayed for their aesthetic charm.

Unpretentious tin articulates all Country styles. Given both ornamental and utilitarian uses, tin is cut, hammered, punched, and crimped into endless distinct shapes. Left untreated, it is discreet, blending effortlessly

with the other elements in a home. When rusted or painted as in tole ware, it demands more attention.

Durable pewter, an alloy of tin, was the material of choice for everyday household utensils from plates to bowls, cups, saucers, and even beer steins until the late eighteenth century, when it was replaced by pottery and china.

✪ (Above) Wrought-iron hardware adds character to a simple pine cupboard with chicken wire covering the door openings. The warm natural wood becomes an effective background for the cool metal corner brace and sliding latch. ✪ (Left) Hotel "silver" is made of a heavy silverplate that will not easily dent. Vintage pieces might have the name on the hotel and even the room number engraved on both service and flatware. It is sought after by Country lovers for its chunky style and nostalgia.

Carved Wood

✪ (Above) Five carved-wood eagles in the dining room represent the most common patriotic symbol used in carving. Many were adapted from the great seal of the United States; but with the typical originality and vigor of the wood carver, others express their personal vision of the eagle. Both realistic and stylized eagles are used on mirror and picture frames, over mantels, as pediments on furniture, and as stand-alone sculpture. As ships' figureheads, they were guardian spirits.

Crafted Metal

Three-dimensional metal weather vanes are quintessential Country design, starting with a dollop of Yankee ingenuity and then merging practicality with art. Few early examples primitively fashioned of wood, iron, and tin survived, falling victim to the elements. Vanes mimicking figures such as angels, whales, horses, grasshoppers, and eagles pivoted on the rooftops and cupolas of both the homes and barns of prosperous early settlers. In the 1860s, mass production, using elegantly designed finely detailed molds, allowed an unlimited variety of cast-metal forms and subjects. Folk-art creations, both conventional and whimsical permitted by the casting process, took form as door knockers, balustrades, cabinet pulls, and lawn ornaments, and are still highly sought after. Time-tested designs, some using the original molds, remain in production today.

✪ (Above) A beloved trotting horse, rotates in the wind, because it has been balanced by filling the front portion of its interior with lead. ✪ (Upper right) The squirrel boasts a powdered verdigris finish over copper. ✪ (Lower right) A cast-iron owl head is used decoratively on an outside door. The hinged head serves as a knocker.

Wire Accents

Wire accents are often used in Country decorating schemes, especially those out-of-doors. Wire, with its rusted finish, ability to be painted, ease of maneuverability, and its low cost made it the perfect material for those who pioneered America. Wire is a substance that originally was used mostly in informal surroundings and largely because of its strength and durability. However, today it has been produced in more ornate Victorian style designs.

A whimsical wire-frame settee, shown at upper left, is the focal point of a secluded retreat in a quiet section of the garden visited by few. The graceful fan-shaped back, double stretcher for support, and scroll design give a satisfying sense of style. The settee plays off against the lush green of the cosmos leaves behind.

Scale, color, and texture must be given the same consideration when planning an outdoor space as when designing an indoor room. Country gardens tend to be casual with plants spilling out of pots, shown to the right of the settee. Plants growing profusely are seldom tamed.

A wire ball surrounded by stone balls at a garden edge, shown at lower right, is fashioned from barbed wire. With over 700 designs for barbed wire receiving patents during the nineteenth century, some variations are more pliable, allowing the talented wireworker to shape them into forms. This sphere, two feet in diameter, attracts birds, who move in and out of the open mesh. The orb has endured as a garden sculpture.

ℬronze Sculpture

Traditional life-sized cast-bronze sculpture, as shown at right, adds texture and a sense of strength to a Country wooded setting, while seeming to blend the boundary between inside and out. Even when the bronze has been given a dark gray patina it remains somewhat reflective, catching the sun as it bounces off the sheen of the hosta and sedum leaves below.

During the winter months, when the trees are bare, the sculpture takes on a different look. Framed by tree trunks and branches, its visual strength is even more apparent and uplifting.

Fashioning a garden sculpture after a member of the family expresses a love of family, while intensifying individuality. No matter what the weather, this sturdy sculpture will endure.

The ancient lost-wax method of casting bronze is a technique that has been employed for over 6,000 years. After an artist has created an original carved from wood, clay, stone, or even another metal, the piece is covered with rubber to make a negative mold.

When the rubber mold has dried, hot wax is painted on the inside to become a positive mold. This wax piece, which replicates the original, is covered with a ceramic shell. When liquid bronze is poured into the ceramic shell, the wax melts. After the metal has cooled, the ceramic shell is broken away. The result is a bronze sculpture exactly like the original.

Country Collections

Stone Fruit

Marble and alabaster stone fruit can be grouped on tables, bowls, shelves, or in a spare row on the mantel.

Most were crafted in Italy beginning in the early 1900s until today. The old pieces, which were hand-carved, painted, then baked to seal in the lovely colors, are the most desired. One can find 50 or so pieces available on a typical day on eBay.

A search of the Internet will reveal groups of antique or collectible stone fruit listed at estate auctions. Each group has a lot number and date for bidding. If you cannot afford vintage pieces, which range widely in price with miniature or oversized pieces costing the most, new stone fruit is also available in department stores, gift shops, and on the Internet.

Stone vegetables such as onions, pea pods, and asparagus are rare. Nuts and watermelon slices are scarce. Apples, oranges, pears, grapes, and figs are easiest to find.

⭐ (Left and above) No matter how pleasing a collection display, it is refreshing to rearrange the elements from time to time.

Tea Leaf Patterned Ironstone

Tea Leaf is one of many ironstone patterns popular with collectors. The Tea Leaf design is a particularly sought-after pattern and inspired the forming of an international club, Tea Leaf Club International, founded in 1980, with nearly 1,000 members in the United States and Canada.

Ironstone was first introduced in Staffordshire, England, around the end of the eighteenth and the beginning of the nineteenth centuries and sold as a durable, inexpensive variety of chinaware, with export exclusively to the United States and Canada. In 1813, Charles James Mason patented an improved china, "harder than earthenware and stronger than porcelain," called "Mason's Patente Ironstone China." When the patent expired fourteen years later, potters, who had been experimenting with similar formulas, began producing it, with many other designs for decoration.

Considered a Country icon, the Tea Leaf design remains the most popular and was used on family tables for over 150 years. There are over 115 body styles.

Miniature Sheep

At the beginning of the twentieth century, tiny sheep were made as part of a Putz scene, which was a village advertised for use at the bottom of a Christmas tree. On the inside of a painted white wooden leg with a black hoof, the name "Germany" appears in purple or red. Those manufactured in Japan were labeled accordingly. An assortment of animals, including sheep, were listed in the 1912 Marshal Field catalog. Later in the 1920s and 1930s they were marked with a round blue and white paper label, "Made in Germany."

✪ (On page 112) Collecting miniature lambs, usually from two to four inches tall, is synonymous with Country. Look about an inviting Country home. Chances are a flock of these diminutive woolly creatures will be found artfully arranged in graduating sizes on a shelf, mantel, or behind the glass doors of a secretary. Early in the century, small sheep and lambs sold for very small change by street vendors in both Europe and America. ✪ (Above and right) A large collection of sheep can be displayed at one time by using simple wooden shelves.

ꝓincushions

Pincushions make a wonderful "small space" collection. Arranging a collection requires order and composition with careful attention given to line, texture, color, size, shape, and theme. There must be a sympathy between objects. Sometimes it is a matter of trial and error. An area may be arranged and then rearranged before it looks right.

Displayed on an antique shelf, shown at upper right, along with other mellow antiques, five pincushions become a cohesive group. Similar but not quite the same, the pincushions are made from scraps of wool fabric. Two are mounted on glass bases converted from hurricane lamps, one on a wine glass, one in a little ceramic cup, and the fifth is made in the shape of a small pillow without a base.

Textile fanciers easily become passionate collectors of antique pincushions. The small scraps of fabric may have been all that remained of a handsome nineteenth-century coarse wool or wool-and-linen blanket. Raw wool and flax had been spun into yarn, woven on handlooms, and dyed with natural pigments giving them muted colors and the appeal of the handmade.

Simple patterns, shown at right, such as stripes, plaids, and checkers were made by alternating yarns of several colors. Because pincushions are made from scraps and are often mounted on a variety of glass bases, two are seldom alike. Even the shapes of the pincushions are varied to include round, oval, cone, pineapple, rectangular, and square pillow forms. Sometimes a small ball of wax for needle storage is attached to the glass base.

✪ Antique pincushions (above) are displayed on an antique wall shelf that was originally a fireplace mantel in a Kentucky home. Each of the pincushions exhibits an individuality both in its shape and variety of fabrics used. The single brass candlestick, 1823 alphabet sampler, pile of leather-bound books, and well-worn pewter plate complete the harmonious scene.

Millinery Heads

The enjoyment of adding to a collection, piece by piece, must be experienced to be understood. A sharp eye is needed to find something personally unique. Perhaps a hat form, like the simply carved head with a stern face, shown at right, in a Shaker museum, will bring smiles. Difficult to resist is the lovely shape of a wooden hat form discovered at a flea market. From the moment of purchasing the first piece, the collection has begun.

Millinery heads with faces delight collectors with amusing expressions and rustic attire. These, shown above, were inspired by antique French forms. Heads and hat forms can be used to display hats or as a mold to shape a hat. Many are wooden forms in definite sizes or those that can be adjusted. Antique wooden hat forms from the nineteenth century are occasionally found in antique shops and may be listed in an auction. They were also made of steel, aluminum, wire, papier-mâché, or even a stiff buckram fabric. Some modern fabric artists use antique hat forms to mold their new hats. The work of one contemporary artist featuring millinery heads was called "unlikely sculpture" when on exhibit at an art museum.

✪ (Left) A mixture of materials can harmoniously be displayed in the same corner because of the folk-art aspect of each.

116

$\mathcal{F}$olk Art

For a uniquely individual collection, consider gathering pieces of American folk art. Without formal academic training, folk artists create work with qualities of vigor and an ability to express themselves that is direct and intimate. The original American folk-art tradition began in the early colonies was recognized in the 1920s, and remains important today.

No two folk-art collections are exactly the same. The concrete soldier, shown on page 116, is very much at home with the two pond boats, complex Ferris wheel, and carved-wood hand, holding a baton.

An 1890s Odd Fellows Hall plaque from Iowa, shown at right, hangs on the wall above intricately carved wooden walking sticks. In times past, a walking stick was essential for formal attire. A snake or serpent surrounding the shaft was a much used theme. Some were weapons with a slender sword concealed in their shafts.

A 1920 ventriloquist's dummy, shown below, hangs next to a cabinet filled with carved human faces and animal figures from the late 1800s to the 1920s.

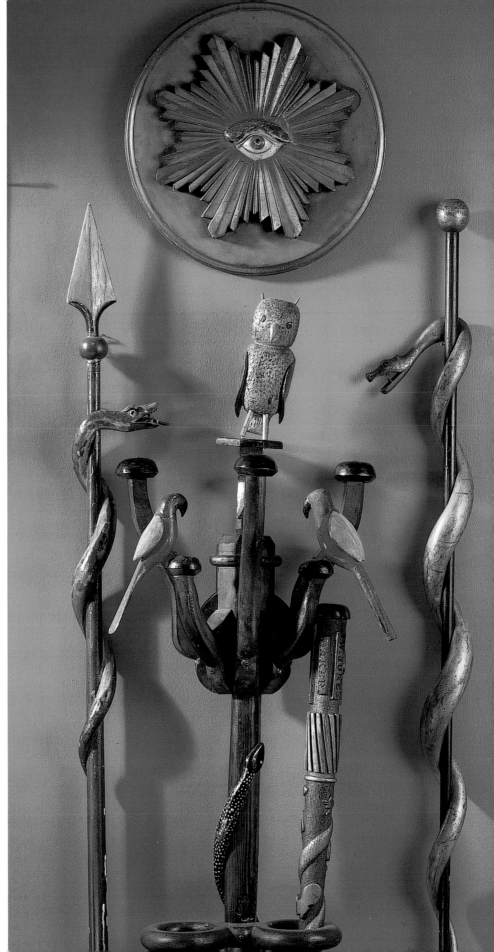

$\mathcal{B}$lock Optic Depression Glass

During the Great Depression, glass dishes were given as premiums by movie theaters and merchants and sold by mail-order houses and five-and-ten-cent stores. They were cheap, machine-molded pieces produced from the mid 1920s into the 1940s, some pieces selling for as little as three cents. In recent years, Depression glass has become very popular with collectors. It can be found in antique malls, country bazaars, and specialty shows featuring collectible glass.

✪ (On page 118) Block Optic Depression glass, mass-manufactured from 1929 to 1933, can be used to set a nostalgic Country table. In addition to green it was made in pink, yellow, crystal, and some amber and blue. ✪ Depression glass was made in more than 95 patterns, such as (above) Manhattan, (below) Moderntone, and (right) Jane Ray, and in green, pink, yellow, white, crystal, amber, and blue—more than 25 colors in all —transparent, translucent, and opaque.

$\mathcal{G}$ames

Board games grouped on a wall have strong visual impact with their geometric designs and lively colors. Multicolored game boards became available after 1839 when lithography came into use making mass-printing practical. Even though over 90 million Monopoly games have been sold they are a perennial favorite for collectors. Was Charles Darrow, an unemployed engineer, the inventor in 1934 or is it an adaptation of a 1904 game called The Landlord? This question may never be answered. The first large-scale edition of Monopoly was issued by Parker Brothers in 1935. Collectible games can be found in second-hand shops, flea markets, and antique shops.

Nests of wooden apples with a warm worn patina, made in Japan and Germany during the 1940s and 1950s, came in graduated sizes with four or five in a set. Although rare, sometimes they contain a small toy, spinning top, or game. They can be found more easily in antique malls and Country antique shops rather than through antique and vintage toy dealers. Complete nesting sets are scarce. Apples containing miniature toy surprises are extremely hard to find and the most costly.

✪ (Right) Scarce and costly wooden apples can be viewed in random assortments along with these antique books.

Boats

A love for the water can be shown by a collection of boats. Boats are best displayed against plain backgrounds that do not detract from the boats themselves, such as a simple custom cabinet with individual compartments for each boat.

Toy boats come in many shapes and sizes and can be quite colorful. Methods of displaying boats are limited only by one's imagination.

Since boats were one of man's earliest means of transportation, toy boats have been popular with children and adults for many generations. They have been made from both wood and metal, even cast iron for "carpet toy boats."

Some manufacturers of toy boats were R. Bliss Mfg. Co., Pawtucket, R. I. (1832–1914), Gebbruder Bing, Nuremburg, Germany (1866–1933), and George W. Brown & Co., Forrestville, Connecticut (1856–1880).

Quite possibly the most outstanding collection of toy boats in existence is that of Malcolm Forbes on the ground floor of the Forbes Publishing Building in New York City (admission is free).

✪ (On page 122) A clever wall of shelves is ideal in displaying these valuable boats. Others added around the room only increase the visual effect. A custom-built cabinet with cubicles displays a fleet of small toy boats, along with larger toy sailboats on its top. The red-hulled 1930s pond boat "floats" with the help of translucent fishing line. ✪ (Below) Rare tin "penny toy" boats from the 1920s and 1930s, include steamboats, a side paddler, rowboats, and a kayak. ✪ (Right) this prized 1930s Pond Yacht was found by the collectors after a two-year search.

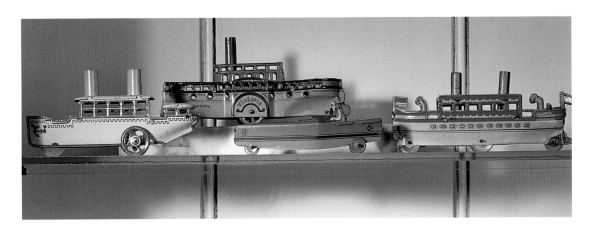

Outdoor Country

Outdoors

The out-of-doors is as much a part of country living and decorating as is the inside of the home. The design for total outdoor living and enjoyment often includes open porches. It is on an outdoor porch where instead of dreaming of a lazy day, you can live it while curled up in a white wicker chair. Once used for occasional get-togethers or parties, open porches have become an entirely separate room in which to relax, play, or even work. Fresh air, moonlit skies, and breathtaking scenery make this the favored room of the house. Family and friends will gather to watch sailboats drift by, enjoy a birthday celebration, or delight in the sounds of children playing on the white sandy beach. Whether celebrating with friends or reading a good book, the simplistic and classic style of an open porch is guaranteed to bring peaceful smiles.

A simple supper or a tall glass of iced tea is enjoyed more under a romantic white gazebo. Thoughtfully placed, it will showcase the Country garden that has been worked on for so long. Graceful patterned and designed wicker furniture, topped off with a crisp white lace tablecloth will intensify the allure of the magical space. Surrounding trees, shrubs, and the fragrant smell of flowers will enclose residents and guests in a secret garden.

✪ (On page 128) Something about fresh air heightens the senses, making a picnic in the garden a mystical experience. Even a tiny garden will provide a romantic spot for a picnic table and chairs. ✪ (Above) Place a rocking chair with a favorite pillow for added comfort. Weathered tables hold a cool drink and bowl of your favorite fruit, while the Country birdhouse will bring friendly feathered visitors. The weathered look of garden furniture adds texture and life to a thoughtful place. ✪ (Upper right) This rustic wooden bench spells Herbs. ✪ (Lower right) Create a place to relax on your private garden deck. An old church pew, painted blue, is the perfect cozy spot for two. A personal touch has been added by surrounding the bench with pots of Peruvian lilies, lavateras, fuscia, and dianthus.

Walled Courtyard

Walled courtyards are a fairly new aspect of outdoor country decorating. They are needed today to muffle the sounds of a busy city, or to secure the privacy once enjoyed by those who lived a country life in the wide open spaces.

A salvaged blue gate gives character to the secluded walled courtyard, shown to the left. The natural latticework will encourage climbing plants.

Similar to the open porch without a protective roof, this narrow walled courtyard, shown below, is open to the sky where friends and family stargaze on a cool summer evening or simply sit and chat. Comfortable cushioned benches placed next to the cedar fence are surrounded by flowers.

*C*ontainer Garden

The garden is an essential element of a Country home. When space is limited, plant a container garden. The fun is working in the soil and tending the plants. Old wheelbarrows make great small space gardens. They can be moved to make the most of sun or shade. Large buckets, baskets with liners, urns, narrow window boxes, vintage metal plant stands, and stoneware crocks work well, too. Consider planting flowers, herbs, or vegetables in a small-space garden.

$\mathcal{P}$orches

A screened porch is a quiet retreat which will function as a true room; a continuation of indoor space. It may remind one of a grandmother's Country home, where it became the place for summer dining or hours on the swing with a friend.

Horsehair was the original screen material to protect from bugs. Today there is a choice of aluminum in black, dark gray, or bright metal. Bronze, copper, brass, and stainless-steel screening as well as plastic is also available. Black is best for visibility from the inside and a clear view out.

Open porches offer an unobstructed look to the yard and, perhaps, the street beyond.

✪ (On page 132) The open porch, with its gray painted floor and white woven-wicker furniture, is on the front of an 1884 house where one can watch the world pass by. ✪ (Below right) A repainted music stand holds a vintage birdhouse. Antique watering cans, a turn of the century cabinet with beaded-board doors, a wicker chair with a quilted seat cushion, and a metal bed frame contribute to the Country charm of the open porch.

133

*B*irdhouses

Birdhouses on poles adjacent to the patio will attract wild birds throughout the warm months. As an accessory they amplify the Country mood of an outdoor space.

Both old and new echo the styles and shapes of houses, churches, and even general stores. One might resemble a shabby Victorian mansion, others a Swiss chalet, rustic barn, or country farmhouse. The style varieties are almost endless.

The sizes of the entry holes and the birdhouse will attract different birds. There are dovecote and martin houses, as well as those for woodpeckers, bluebirds, wrens, finches, flickers, and more. Materials vary from natural untreated lumber, to stained or painted hardwoods, recycled driftwood and hollow gourds.

When coming upon another birdhouse that strikes a fancy, it is easy to add it to a porch or garden. The look says Country and a home becomes even more personal with each added birdhouse.

When grouping birdhouses on the porch, against a wall, or in an open outdoor space, think of creating an elegant still life. The common theme linking them together will make them easy to arrange.

✪ (Upper left on page 135) A family of small weathered birdhouses hung from a porch roof on almost invisible wires, becomes a pleasing display. ✪ (Upper right on page 135) The wall behind the birdhouses is an effective backdrop. ✪ (Below on page 135) Five rustic bird-houses of similar design in the farm garden create an appealing composition.

Salvage

Give discarded pieces of furniture a second life. A collection of antique syrup pitchers will hang jauntily on a rusting garden gate. A vintage iron bed painted white, as shown at lower left, will give any flower garden a sense of fun. A basket of blooms may work well with that rustic chair missing its seat.

The nearby farmhouse being torn down may yield interesting treasures. Remember some else's discards can be just right for the Country home. Try to "hang loose" while shopping. You cannot predict how many times a salvage warehouse needs to be explored before finding just the right thing.

ℬirdbaths

Strategically place birdbaths on decks, patios, or in the garden where they can be enjoyed from the breakfast or dining table. Birdbaths are lovely for a small space. Watching birds splashing about in cool water brings one of the joys of nature even closer.

Made from antique brass, cast aluminum, terracotta, sandstone, concrete, and resin, birdbaths come in many designs from classic Williamsburg, Venetian, Victorian, Lotus Leaf, modern, and Monticello—the latter design replicates the birdbath at Thomas Jefferson's Virginia home. They can be placed on the ground, perched on a pedestal, or mounted onto a deck rail.

Birds like water that moves so consider a birdbath with a fountain at its edge or in the center. The fountain can be an abstract shape, a small sundial in the shape of a pineapple, or a flower. The water should not be more than three inches deep. Birds like to rub across the rough bottom. Set the bath in partial shade close to trees and shrubs for an after-bathing shake.

Watering Cans

Watering cans are not just for watering. Watering cans or pots have come a long way since the early earthenware pot with a perforated base used in Italy in the sixteenth century. Lead-glazed earthenware pots with large perforated roses appeared during the seventeenth century, followed by brass and copper pots during the eighteenth century. Early nineteenth-century tinplate pots were often painted red or green. Rust-resistant galvanized-steel watering cans are available in a vast variety of shapes and sizes to meet every kind of gardening need.

✪ (Upper left) A sturdy oval-shaped can with shallow grip houses a kitty. ✪ (Below left) Mosquitoes cannot breed in collected water if cans hang upside down on a rustic wooden post. ✪ (Below) Six collectible watering cans on a potting bench become a vase for cut flowers.

✪ (Above) Four galvanized-steel cans lined on the steps make excellent planters. The perforated roses have been removed from these four. ✪ (Upper right) They can be displayed like the eight cans on the shelf above the door, or simply used for their intended purpose—to give a drink to garden plants. ✪ (Lower right) Cans with both handles and a grip are the easiest to carry and manipulate without spilling their contents.

Gates

Gates have always been an important part of outdoor country. Fences are used in wide open spaces between country homes to define the property lines and to secure each individual's privacy. A white picket fence and a garden gate can be used as a boundary to divide areas within a garden. An open gate says, "Welcome. Do come in," whereas a closed gate discourages trespassers.

There are thousands of sites on the Internet where you can shop for arbors, pergolas, fences, and gates. They are available in a variety of styles and built from woods including pressure-coated cedar, redwood, cypress, teak, cedar logs, and bentwood twigs.

Some are constructed of powder-coated wrought iron or steel, aluminum, metal mesh, and hollow copper tubing, which will oxidize to a blue-green.

Wooden Arbors

Intricate garden arbors are a wonderful way to achieve a Country look. Their skeletal forms will add excitement to a garden as the soft feel of the green plants and the hard surface of the arbor interact. Arbors, originally intended to tame unruly plants and vines, will work well even in a restricted space.

When planning an outdoor space, the approach should be very much the same as designing a room. Begin by dreaming a little. Envision an inviting garden—an extension of a home that will feel casual and congenial, one that will offer a fresh way of seeing things.

Next, consider the family's lifestyle. Will it require quiet privacy or frequent entertaining for large groups of friends? Now take another look at the garden. Imagine how it will look with arbors as a backdrop for blooming flowers or visualize a seat for relaxation.

Shop at a local garden furniture store and on the Internet to find out more about the arbor sizes and designs available. Sketching plans to determine the scale and placement of arbors is a must. There is a thrill and satisfaction when paper plans become reality.

$\mathcal{A}$cknowledgments

Bed & Breakfasts

Eagle Center House, Eagle, Wisconsin 110–111

Maison Fleurie, Yountville, California 22–23

White Lace Inn, Sturgeon Bay, Wisconsin . . . . .127 (lower)

Antique Dealers

Robert Strauss and Steven Stout, Ann Arbor, Michigan . . . . .12, 56, 58, 81, 114 (upper), 135

Mary DeBuhr, Downers Grove, Illinois 6–7, 96–97, 106–107, 112

Marion Atten, (Antiques at Hillwood Farm), Pecatonica, Illinois 13

Pat Schroeder, Eagle, Wisconsin . . . . .2–3, 30, 54–55, 59 (lower right), 83

Joan Lucas, High Ridge, Missouri . . . . .14, 33 (far right), 47 (lower right)

Marti Diederich, Yorkville, Illinois 15

Richard Peterson and Frank Colvin, Lanark, Illinois . . . . .9 (lower), 77, 82

Jan Carroll, Lanark, Illinois 86

Cindy Lain, Paducah, Kentucky 98

Joanne Babb,(The Potting Shed), Libertyville, Illinois . . . . .1, 44–45, 50–51, 106–107, 108–109, 121 (lower)

Paula & Tom Van Deest, Cedar Rapids, Iowa 116–117

Anne & Chuck Bruser, West Chicago, Illinois 102

Manufacturer

Alpine Log Homes, Victor, Montana 4–5, 16–17, 10–11

Artisans and Craftspeople

The Workshops of David T. Smith, Morrow, Ohio 28–29, 32, 39, 72–73, 76, 122

Sue Jones, Cummings, Georgia . . . . .26, 47 (upper right)

Peggy Teich, Elm Grove, Wisconsin . . . . .47 (lower right)

Marsha Van Valin, Sullivan, Wisconsin 8, 60

Kate Tully, Prospect Heights, Illinois . . . . .64 (lower)

Joyce Pahlier, Green Bay, Wisconsin 68–69

Laura Chapell and Barbara Fisher (Follow Your Heart), Denver, Colorado 70–71

Steven Shelton, Vienna, Missouri 115

Gayla Bailey, Georgetown, Indiana ....33 (lower left), 41–43, 135 (lower)

Mary Radke, Yorkville, Illinois ....59 (upper right), 85

Photo Stylist

Nina Williams, Denver, Colorado ....Page 16–17, 70–71

Home Owners

Gayla & Tom Bailey, Alice & Robert Biggers, Gaye & Bob Bowers, Marjorie Busch, Marcia & Tom Busym, Sheridan & Arbold Cernick, Candy Cleveland, Linda Coffey, Bailey Davis, Lisa DeFaccio & Jim Biel, Helen & Steve Guittard, Marilyn & Ken Haley, Sally & Herbert Loeb, Tami & Bryan Martin, Pam & Larry Masse, Lorel & Robert MacMillan, Anetta & James Nagell, Helen & William Obrocta, Diane & John Patience, Mary & Bill Radke, Josie & Ron St. Louis, Susie & George Spiel, Sue & Rip Suster, Sherri & James Swinehart, Merrill Taylor, Trudi Temple, Mary & Bert Turek

About the Author

Jessie Walker is a renowned International assignment and stock photographer who devotes much of her time to photographing homes and gardens for publication in national magazines. She has photographed worldwide on assignment throughout the United States and in England, France, Germany and Norway. Her photography of places and people in India, Thailand, and Burma has become a part of corporate design. Her photography has been the subject of one-man shows at the Chicago Press Club, the Chicago Athletic Club, Ruth Volid Gallery, and the Zenith Corporate headquarters. Jessie's work is part of the permanent collection of the Museum of Contemporary Photography, Chicago. The Museum named her as the best photographer of interiors in the area and honored her in a special exhibition *Target Market.*

Her photography has been published in over 100 hardcover books. She is the author and photographer of *Country Living Collectibles— Rabbits* published in 1996 and her photography was featured in a short segment for PBS Television.

Even though Jessie holds both Bachelor and Masters degrees in journalism from Northwestern University, her true love is photography.

She is a member of the American Society of Media Photographers and lives in Glencoe, Illinois, with her husband Arthur Griggs.

Index